Contents

Introduction

ha-ppy-ist

noun: happyist; plural noun: happyists

>	a person who is a happy specialist

>	a person who is happier than most

I am a self-proclaimed happyist - I love to be happy and to make others happy. My glass is always half full, I can spot a silver lining from a mile away, and my rose-colored glasses are permanently affixed. There are numerous benefits of being a happyist – we are healthier, less-stressed, and live longer than our miserable counterparts (according to healthline.com) - and I invite you to try it for yourself. In my happy opinion, you will never look back.

My goal in writing this book is to empower others to create habits and learn behaviors that will allow them to live happier lives. There are countless ways to be happy, and happiness may mean something different to each of us, but I will introduce you to a few so you may begin the journey to becoming a happyist. Some of these may resonate more with you than others, but I sincerely hope that something you read will strike a chord within you and inspire action.

The last chapter of the book, "Be happy, healthy and kind one day at a time," is based on daily themes that are intended to be put into action and repeated indefinitely. The theory behind this concept is that these three mindsets (happy, healthy, and kind) feed off each other, and as one area improves, so does the next. In other words: as we become happier, we become healthier in other areas of our lives. As we become happier and healthier, we find it easier to be kinder to others, and this, in turn, leads to more happiness and so on. This portion of the book focuses on a different theme each day that contributes to a long term happyist lifestyle.

My wish is that you enjoy the book, become a life-long happyist, and inspire others to begin a journey to be happy, healthy, and kind.

Chapter 1 – Be your own BESTY

Believe

you are **E**nough

and **S**tay

True

to **Y**ourself

Why you should be your own BESTY

A best friend is kind, loving, supportive, generous, and respectful. A best friend is someone you want to be around constantly; someone you can laugh within the good times and be comforted by in the bad times. Don't rely on someone else to do these things for you. Be your own best friend and give yourself these gifts every single day.

I have found that many people are great friends to others but treat themselves terribly. They say things to themselves they would never dream of saying to a friend or even a stranger. I have heard people say, "I'm so stupid," or "I'm terrible at that," or "I'm such an idiot." They would be appalled if someone else said these same things to them or about them. It is time to recognize that we should treat ourselves as well – if not better – than we treat others. We should be kind, loving, supportive, generous, and respectful to ourselves at all times.

Other people may let you down – whether intentionally or unintentionally – and they cannot always be there for you. However, you can always be there for you. In fact, you can't escape yourself - so it makes perfect sense to be your own besty. Become your own loudest cheerleader, your fiercest protector, and your softest comforter.

I cringe when I hear the expression, "I'm my own worst critic." What an awful thought. Throughout our lives, people, jobs, and things will come and go. The most fortunate of us will be blessed with some incredible people to lean on, but nothing is forever, and we must learn to rely on ourselves and to draw strength from ourselves instead of others. We can hardly do this while being overly critical of ourselves. If we constantly criticize ourselves, we will begin to believe the negative thoughts and doubt our abilities. However, if we encourage and support ourselves, we will begin to believe that we are capable of so much more. If I had my way, I would ban that phrase from the English language and change it to "I'm my own biggest fan."

How to be your own besty:

A best friend is kind – learn to be kind to yourself. Focus on your very best qualities and be patient when your weaknesses surface. None of us are perfect, and we should be as kind to ourselves as we are to others.

A best friend is loving – learn to love yourself. You are an incredible individual. The unique aspects of your personality should be celebrated daily. Spoil yourself as you would spoil a loved one with compliments and appreciation.

A best friend is supportive – learn to support yourself. The most important praise comes from within because only we truly know the effort we put forth. Be proud of your achievements and encourage yourself when the going gets rough.

A best friend is generous – learn to give to yourself as well as to others. We cannot pour from an empty cup and must remember to recharge the batteries that allow us to shine and shower others with blessings.

A best friend is respectful – learn to respect yourself. Create healthy boundaries and politely keep them intact out of self-respect. Become more aware of your aspirations, likes, and dislikes and keep the commitments you make to yourself as well as those you make to others.

My Story

When I tell people the story of how I left England and came to America at the age of 20, they often remark on how incredibly brave I was. It does indeed seem to be a courageous feat. I had never been to America before and didn't know a single person in the entire country. I had never traveled alone, I had never been on an eight-hour flight, and I was a nervous flyer. Nevertheless, I left everything and everyone I knew to go to a foreign country and live with a family I had never met before to care for their children for 12 months.

But the truth is, I was not brave – I was actually a coward. I was more afraid to stay in my life, in England, than I was to move to a different country thousands of miles from my family and friends and all I had ever known.

At that time, I didn't believe I was smart enough to go to college and grew miserable when all my friends left to start their new lives at various universities around the country. I was still living at home and didn't believe I was strong enough to move out on my own, although I desperately wanted to escape my dysfunctional family. I had fallen head over heels for a great guy who treated me well, but I didn't believe I was lovable enough for him to want to stick around for long. I had a decent job and the potential for a long-term career with a stable company, but I didn't believe I was good enough to be successful.

So, rather than facing any of these issues, I chose to "run away" from my life to a place where nobody knew me, and nobody knew that I wasn't enough.

Over the next two decades, I gradually found my strength, my confidence, and myself. During those years, I made many mistakes: I married and divorced the wrong person; developed and overcame a drinking problem; and stayed in a job because I didn't know how to do anything else. I now love my life, and I love myself, and I KNOW that I am enough. My path was a painful one, and it took many years for me to become my own besty. I made some terrible choices along the way because I didn't love myself, and I now want to help others on their journey. I don't want you to wait two decades to figure out that you are enough because you ARE. It's a miracle that you are even here. There is a one in 400 trillion chance that you were born at all, and of the 7.7 billion people alive on the planet, you are the only you. There is nobody else quite like you. You are unique in your talents and abilities and what you can offer the world. You are most certainly enough, and there is a profound reason for your existence – you are here to serve others and make a difference with your incredible gifts.

Your story

Your story may be different from mine. I was raised by a mother who – to this day – has zero coping skills, and every problem she encounters sends her into a spiral of negative emotions. Consequently, I mirrored her, as most of us mirror our early role models, and I had no clue as to how I should cope with anything life threw at me. Worse yet – I dreaded the unknown because I feared I wasn't equipped to handle any hardship. In addition to this, my stepfather was a violent tyrant who didn't allow us to have opinions or make decisions, and I became a "pleaser" because I was terrified of upsetting him (and later anyone else).

Of course, the chances that you were raised by an emotional wreck and a tyrant are slim, but the chances are strong that you were raised in an equally or even more damaging environment. Perhaps you were repeatedly told you would never be good enough, or perhaps you were simply never told you were already good enough. We all have sad stories to varying degrees, and many people reading this may be more damaged than I can ever imagine. To those people, I offer the simple truth – that you ARE enough, that you DO matter, and that you are here for a reason – and I pray that you will choose to believe it now and forevermore.

The good news is that you can decide how your story will end. You can begin to believe that you are enough and learn to stay true to yourself. By doing so, you will not only create your own happy ending, but you will also create a happy ending for many generations to come because you will be a positive role model.

Once we believe we are enough, the next step is to stay true to ourselves. Although both steps are difficult, it is perhaps hardest to complete this second step. This is often because those who have never believed in themselves rarely dream about their own path and choices. We need to first understand ourselves and learn more about what makes us unique.

We must devote time to reflect on our aspirations and goals. Throughout our lives, we are led one way or another by the thoughts of what we "should" or "shouldn't" do, according to others who have influenced us – our parents, friends, teachers, or even the media.

I was determined that my children would attend university immediately after high school because I didn't find the conviction to do it until I turned 40. Throughout their lives, I lectured them on the benefits of higher education and even assured them I would happily pay for it so they wouldn't have any excuse. During my oldest son's senior year in high school, he finally admitted to me, after months of heated discussions on the topic, that he just wanted to work in construction like his dad. I was devastated and kept asking myself where I had gone wrong. What had I said – or not said – that made him reach this decision? What could I now do to help him see the error of his ways? Today, three years after graduating, he is a homeowner and a happy and well-adjusted 21-year-old with a clear vision for a successful future that works for HIM – not me. I am grateful that he is content and that he taught me a valuable lesson by being brave enough to stay true to himself.

So, the question is: how do we know which path to follow? Especially if we have not previously considered this due to not believing we are enough to choose? Aristotle said: "Knowing yourself is the beginning of all wisdom."

We can only be the very best version of ourselves when we are true to ourselves. We cannot be truly happy when we live somebody else's version of our life. It may take many years to determine what our truth is, but along the way, we are often pretty sure of what it isn't. When faced with a dilemma or a fork in the road, it is often easier to decide which path is wrong rather than which is right. Trust your instincts to help you find your truth. That sickening feeling in your stomach is there for a reason, and if something doesn't feel "right," – it probably isn't. If you dread something, it is most likely not meant for you, but if you have genuine excitement, it certainly is.

I think we often ignore these feelings because we feel we "have to" or "should" do certain things. But ignoring the signs prolongs the agony of living a life that isn't true to ourselves. By paying attention to the red flags, we are often steered in the right direction – even if we aren't fully aware of the destination. By knowing what we don't want, we may just discover what we do want.

I have known both sides of the coin and can attest to the fact that you will be much more content in a life that is meant for you and that truly satisfies you. Try living the life you were meant to live, and you will find it is the best gift you could ever give yourself as your own BESTY.

Chapter 2 – The ABCs of Positivity

Remaining positive in today's world can be tough. All around us, negativity reigns. The news, social media, and even friends and family present a constant barrage of bad news and reasons to fume. I believe there is an effective method to remaining positive even in the most awful of circumstances. As long as you can remember the first three letters of the alphabet, you can employ this method to stay calm. It is truly that easy.

The ABCs of positivity are:

- Assume good intent
- Believe in the plan
- Choose to be happy

Let's start with the A, which stands for "assume good intent." Have you ever unintentionally wronged someone and tried to apologize, only to find them unforgiving? I have. I generally feel really bad about it too, and just can't believe they won't let it go.

Here's an example: I am driving home from work, on "auto-pilot" after a particularly challenging day and realize I will miss my exit unless I cut across 3 lanes of traffic, narrowly missing several other drivers who are most displeased with my inconsiderate driving. I truly don't mean to upset the other drivers, and I can certainly understand their angry gestures, so I wave an apology and expect them to instantly forgive me – after all, it was a simple mistake.

Here's another example: I am at work, and it's another particularly challenging day (I seem to have a lot of those). I schedule a meeting, and, in my haste, I forget to invite a key staff member. When the staff member realizes I didn't invite them, they jump to all sorts of conclusions about why I didn't invite them: "who does she think she is?"; "she must think she knows it all"; "what am I – chopped liver?" As soon as I see the error,

I quickly extend the invite and expect to be easily forgiven – after all, it was a simple mistake.

I could go on and on about the times I have unintentionally wronged someone – I am far from perfect. But what happens when we are wronged by someone else's simple mistake? Do we forgive others as quickly as we expect to be forgiven? Or do we instantly become enraged and assume the offense was purposeful?

For some reason, we have a tendency to think others are "out to get us" or inconsiderate or rude when they make mistakes. I can't count the times someone has walked through a door before me without holding it open for me to walk through. Many of those times, I have uttered a sarcastic "thank you" under my breath. Rudeness and a lack of common decency rank high on my list of pet peeves. After all, it doesn't cost a single penny to be polite and thoughtful. During these times, I have instantly assumed these people are rude and inconsiderate of others, but recently I did the very same thing, and it was a simple mistake. I was walking through a building completely preoccupied with my thoughts as I hurried from one place to another when I rushed through a door without looking to see if someone was following me. A few steps later, I realized that someone was indeed behind me, and I gushed an apology hoping they would believe me because I would never have intentionally acted so rudely. I'm not sure they believed me, but it made me realize that I was guilty of doing something I had been disgusted by so many times before. It also made me realize that perhaps the people that had allowed doors to close in my face were also preoccupied and truly didn't realize I was there. Finally, it made me realize I had been so quick to assume their bad intent rather than their good intent.

I have committed to the concept of assuming good intent when I am wronged because I have wronged others so many times without bad intent. Therefore, it is entirely possible that those who wrong me have no bad intent. There are certainly rude, abrasive, and inconsiderate people in this world, but there are many, many more of us who are not – at least not intentionally. So, let's work together on assuming people mean no harm towards us, rather than that they do. Let's forgive others as quickly as we would like to be forgiven for the simple mistakes we make all too often. And let's assume good intent. I believe we will be much happier for it.

The B stands for "believe in the plan." As a Christian, I believe that God has a plan for my life that is leading me towards wonderful things. Even in dark times, I am comforted by this belief. You may not share my faith, but instead, believe that "everything happens for a reason." I have heard countless stories of people going through rough times and coming out the other side stronger and even grateful for the struggle. I have heard stories of people faced with a terrible situation only to find that something better was waiting just around the corner for them.

I recently read a book about Steve Harvey, who faced multiple hardships before becoming the famous comedian we know today. He dropped out of University, was laid off, divorced, and became homeless before breaking through in the entertainment industry. A weaker man may have given up the dream after the first set back, but he continued to pursue his purpose and believes that the rough times ultimately led him to his fame.

I have my own stories, and I'm sure you do too. Most of us have them because most of us have struggled at one time or another. But so many times in my life, I have looked back and realized that I was meant to survive the storm to appreciate the rainbow when the sun shone again. One such time was my divorce. As a heartbroken divorced mother of two young boys at the age of 34, I had no idea how to be alone, and even less how to be a single parent. But little did I know that there was a good man in my future who has become my rock. Obviously, this is a drastically simplified version of my story, which contains highs and lows and twists and turns, but I can sincerely look back at those dark years and be thankful that my journey unfolded the way it did. I am now thankful for the darkness, which taught me so much about myself and others. I am now thankful for the pain that allows me to help others in similar situations. And I am now thankful for the life I never would have had without first having the struggle.

When the going gets tough, remember there is a plan for your life. Whether you believe it was ordained by God or the Universe, it exists.

There may be a struggle, but the outcome will far exceed your dreams, and it will be worth it. By believing in the plan, your struggle will be less, and you will find a breakthrough sooner than if you wallow in misery. Allow yourself to be led to your next chapter, and it will reveal itself to you.

The C stands for "choose to be happy." One of my favorite quotes is, "life is ten percent what happens to you and ninety percent how you react to it." Life is going to be good, and it is going to be bad, but, during the good and the bad, we can choose to be happy. This choice allows the good to be great and the bad to be bearable. It allows us to regain control of a situation when life is gloomy by deciding how we are going to act despite hardship, pain, or misery.

When I am wronged, I find it helpful to remember that my reaction is completely up to me. I can be mad/sad/angry, or I can let it go and choose to be happy in spite of the wrong. After all, why would I give another person the satisfaction of upsetting me when I can choose to be happy and not allow their actions to bother me? And why would I give anyone else that kind of power over my life? When I choose to be happy, I can move on and enjoy this precious gift of life, rather than wasting my short time on this earth in sadness.

This may be the most difficult of the three steps because many of us have become so accustomed to the reaction of anger that it is now our automatic reaction. We can reverse this reaction with practice, but we must first be aware of it happening. Starting today, take note of the signs when anger or negativity overtake you so that you can begin to quickly recognize them in the future. Once you are aware of these signals and feelings, you can more effectively reduce your reaction and begin to consciously choose to smile, breathe, and focus on peace and positive thoughts.

I am a huge fan of personal mantras. Mine is "be happy, healthy and kind," and I repeat this to myself when I feel anger or negativity rising as a reaction to someone or something. Feel free to adopt this mantra for yourself or choose another such as "expect nothing and appreciate everything" or "everything I need is within me." I find it calming to repeat my mantra in times of stress, disappointment, anger, and negativity, and I encourage you to try it when you are struggling.

Chapter 3 – Expectations

I am learning to lower my expectations of others – not in a "they are going to disappoint me anyway/I must protect my heart" kind of way – but in a non-judgmental/non-controlling kind of way. My husband is very different from me (think chalk and cheese), and one of our differences is that I am a people pleaser, and he is not. As a people pleaser, I am prone to saying yes to everyone and everything, which drives him crazy. Conversely, he is prone to very easily and very quickly saying no to the majority of requests, which drives me crazy. Neither of us is necessarily right nor wrong, but we have learned over the years to be more understanding of each other when our reactions to a request are different. Instead of stubbornly insisting that my way is the right way, I now make an effort to understand that we are two vastly different people with often two vastly different concepts of the right way.

Let me give you an example. Last year, my brother-in-law attended a special needs prom. It was a much-anticipated event for him and a much-talked-about event in our household. My husband and I both took him, but when it came time for him to be collected, my husband refused to come with me because he was tired and didn't want to make the hour round trip. I was livid. From my perspective, he should not want his wife to have to drive the hour round trip by herself in the dark along country roads – not to mention the fact that it was for HIS brother. From his perspective, I am a perfectly independent and capable woman, and I was the one to suggest his brother attend the event; therefore, I should be the one to be inconvenienced at 10 pm on a Saturday night. I left the house fuming, slamming doors, and refusing to say goodbye. I returned to find my husband sleeping – he was obviously less perturbed than I was by the issue.

Which of us was right in this situation? It certainly would have been nice if he had offered to come with me, but I have no right to assume that he should agree. I realized last Saturday night, as I have done many times during our marriage that we simply see the world differently and that shouting and yelling and enforcing my will is unlikely to change his mind. It is, I have discovered, far more helpful for me to pause and understand that I cannot expect him to react to everything the same way that I do. Just because I think he should want to do something doesn't mean that he actually does want to do it and vice-versa. Just because I would have offered to drive with him at 10 pm on a Saturday night doesn't mean that he should offer to drive with me. When my head cleared, I was able to remember that I am far from perfect, and I am grateful when he accepts my flaws rather than fuss over them, so shouldn't I treat him similarly? I also remembered that I want a husband who is a partner – not one that I can control to suit my needs.

Another example of the benefit of lowering expectations occurred during a company lunch meeting when a colleague couldn't eat the catered meal due to a food allergy. She was upset because the organizer had not taken the time to ask the attendees if they had allergies prior to selecting the caterer. I can certainly sympathize with my colleague in this situation – she was hungry and unable to eat. However, I can also sympathize with the organizer. Most people are not personally affected by food allergies, and therefore don't give much thought to the fact that others may need special considerations in this area. My colleague was visibly upset by this situation for some time and even posted a reference about it on social media later that evening. I wonder if she could have saved herself the anger and upset if she could have assumed the organizer had good intentions, and just because she would have asked attendees about food allergies, it simply did not occur to the organizer. When I am faced with similar circumstances, I am learning to give the benefit of the doubt. Perhaps the organizer was under pressure to submit the catering order quickly or at the last minute. Perhaps the organizer truly assumed there would be something for everyone in the selection she made. I certainly don't think the organizer intentionally selected the food, knowing that my colleague would be unable to eat it. My colleague stewed over this for hours and literally allowed it to ruin her day, but the organizer was oblivious to the issue.

I learned two things from this incident: that I should lower my expectations of others and not assume they would do something purely because I would have; and that there is no point in allowing someone else's actions or inactions to ruin my day when they most likely did not intend any bad will. In retrospect, I also learned a third thing – always have a back-up plan – but that's a discussion for another day.

We cannot expect others to view the world as we do and should allow them the space to be true to themselves rather than be controlled by us. After all, isn't that how we would prefer to be treated?

Chapter 4 – The Best Day Ever

Take a moment to think about the best days of your life. Do they include your wedding day? The day you graduated? The day your child was born? The days spent on a white sandy beach with nothing to worry about but which fruity drink you should choose next? How many "best days" have you had over your lifetime – 10…5…1? How many best days will you have this year, between January 1 and December 31?

I am on track to have 365 best days of my life this year.

You can make every day the best day of your life. And you should. You owe it to yourself, and you owe it to your family, your friends, your colleagues, and everyone you come in contact with. Even complete strangers can benefit from your happiness because you never know when a smile or friendly greeting may help someone who is having a rough time or even experiencing a crisis. There are countless stories of people contemplating suicide whose lives were forever changed after being touched by a stranger's unexpected kindness.   If you knew you had that kind of power, wouldn't you use it? The good news is that you DO have that power, and you SHOULD use it. Every. Single. Day.

You can wake up every morning and decide that the upcoming day will be wonderful. You will be happier and healthier as a result of making this decision. If this sounds too good to be true – IT IS NOT! However, it is NOT easy. I struggle every day to make good choices, including choosing my mood, but it DOES get easier and more natural each time I do it.

Now, I know that life can be incredibly difficult. I have experienced demanding, unpleasant, and downright mean bosses. I have raised teenagers – plural – at the same time – who have an uncanny knack for ruining a good mood with a single slammed door. I have lived through a turbulent marriage, a heartbreaking divorce, single parenthood, and then the challenges of remarriage and blended families.   BUT, on the days I decide to be happy, all of these things (and more) are so much easier to handle. My problems don't go away when I choose joy over anger, sadness, regret, resentment (etc.), but my load feels lighter. When I choose to be happy, despite my challenges, the issues are drastically easier to deal with.

The investment in committing to making this daily choice is incredibly worthwhile. I have personally seen a dramatic improvement in my stress levels and my health in general since making this change. I have seen improvements in my marriage because it's hard to argue with someone who refuses to engage in an argument in case it ruins the best day ever. ("Sorry but I'm having the best day of my life today and I can't allow you to destroy it for me"). There was a time I would have ranted and raved and sulked and pouted during a disagreement that may or may not have lasted for several days (I come from a long line of pouters), but on my best day ever, I simply smile, apologize when needed, and forgive quickly and easily so that I can get back to having the best day ever.

My children's' attitudes have also improved. Even those of us that do not have a degree in psychology know that children tend to mimic their parents' behavior, so doesn't it make sense to exhibit the behavior we want them to adopt? I don't know a single parent that doesn't want happy, healthy, and kind children, so we should strive to be the person they can mirror to achieve this.

This theory also extends to the workplace. Interactions with complaining colleagues leave us feeling miserable and drained, whereas interactions with optimistic co-workers leave us feeling positive and lighthearted. I don't know about you, but I prefer positive over miserable, and I want to spread happiness in a world that has become increasingly angry and negative, but I can only do that when I have first chosen to be happy and positive.

I believe that we can have happier relationships, homes, workplaces, and even communities. And it is not as difficult as you may think. My plan for this is to replace the "**F**" words in your life – frustration, fury, fear (there may be others) – with these:

- **Find** the positive – there is always, always something to be thankful for. We don't have to go far to find someone that is worse off than ourselves. Every day we wake up is a fresh start to live a fulfilling life. Also, find the positive people in your life – not only are they more pleasant to be around, but we also tend to become more like the people we spend time with.

- **Focus** on others –we gain so much by helping others, not least of which is joy. According to *Psychology Today*, "experiments have demonstrated again and again that kindness toward others actually causes us to be happier, improves our health and lengthens our lives."   That's a win-win-win.

- **Fake** it until you make it – when all else fails, you really can fool yourself into feeling happy by pretending to feel happy. You may have heard or read that new habits are created in 21 days, commit to making a habit of being happy. What better habit could you create, than one which helps you become happy? Like any habit, it will eventually become second nature. I promise it works. Try it.

So, when life gets tough, choose to be happy anyway. When someone wrongs you, choose to be happy anyway. When ______ (fill in the blank) happens to you, choose to be happy anyway. You can choose your emotions. You can make the conscious choice to remain happy despite life's problems. Don't give anybody else that much power over your life. Especially not the people who treat you poorly – they don't deserve your energy, time, or emotions. And they certainly don't deserve to take the credit for ruining the best day of your life. Only you can control your feelings because they belong to you only.

Have the best day of your life today and, while you're at it, you will help others have their best day too.

Chapter 5 – Sparkle

Do you know anyone that sparkles? I'm referring to the kind of person that lights up a room, the kind of person that you enjoy being around because they lift your mood, the kind of person that attracts others effortlessly.

When I think of famous sparklers, Ellen DeGeneres comes to mind immediately because she is always smiling, bubbly, light and bright, and kind. There are many others – Will Smith and Oprah are two of the more famous ones. But I have also been lucky enough to know a few real-life sparklers, and I have realized they share some common traits.

Here are my thoughts on how we can all sparkle:

S – smile

Sparklers seem to smile MUCH more than the general population, and their contagious smiles are one of the reasons we love to be around them. Do the sparklers smile because they are happy, or are they happy because they smile? There is a theory, which I wholeheartedly agree with, that smiling in itself is a short cut to happiness because the brain believes we are happy when it gets the signal that we are smiling. Once the brain thinks we are happy, it works at making the happiness real for us. So, smile more. At the very least, you will be more pleasant to be around, and you just might be happier for it.

P – positive

The sparklers' positive outlook is their superpower. A sparkler's glass is always half full, and their rose-colored glasses are permanently affixed. This trait can be adopted by deciding to focus on the good around us. Tony Robbins (the world-famous motivational speaker) demonstrated that we see what we choose to see with a simple exercise. He told a room of people to look for as many red objects they could find within ten seconds, then after they frantically counted, he asked them how many blue items they saw. The crowd wasn't able to identify any blue objects because they had been so focused on finding red ones. This shows us that we find what we are looking for and that we can find more positivity by simply focusing on it.

A – appreciate

A sparkler appreciates life and all its blessings. They fully embody the expression "gratitude is the best attitude," and they often surprise us by finding the silver linings that are invisible to others. It is said that no other emotion can be felt when we are truly grateful for something. This is one you can practice anywhere and anytime – just think of something or someone you are thankful for and feel the anger, stress, and negativity melt away. We can train ourselves to recognize those pesky bad thoughts as they appear and then switch our focus to something we appreciate. Perhaps in time, this habit will become as natural as it seems to be for our sparkler friends.

R – rejoice

Sparklers don't just enjoy an occasion – they rejoice in it. They celebrate at a higher level than most, and they do so more often than most. This is another behavior that can become habitual over time if we make an effort to adopt it by paying attention to the many opportunities we have to celebrate. Like most positive traits, it becomes easier with time to rejoice in the little things. I have a friend who loves to "high five." She will raise her hand at the slightest hint of good news, which would be off-putting if it weren't for the fact that her delight is so genuine that I find my hand raising to meet hers without a second thought.

K – kindness

I think a sparkler's kindness may be their energy source. Their good deeds are like the flame that ignites their firework namesakes. The kindness is never forced or at least doesn't appear to be, and it is given generously and frequently. They embody the adage that kindness benefits the giver as much as the receiver because they seem far happier than the general population.

L – listen

One of the ways a sparkler makes others feel special is by listening. They seem to do a lot less talking than many people, and a conversation with a sparkler leaves us feeling heard, understood, and cared for. If you know a sparkler, think of a time when you have talked to them – would you agree that they exhibit this trait? The sparklers in my life seem to understand why we were given two ears and only one mouth.

E – encourage

A sparkler is a natural cheerleader – one who happily points out the good work done by others and makes the rest of us want to do more of it. Sparklers radiate support and love. They motivate others to reach for the stars and make us believe that anything is possible. Like all sparkler traits, this one can be easily adopted and should be shared with others because encouragement builds confidence where it is lacking and inspires hope on dark days.

Chapter 6 – Enjoy the journey

I have recently embraced the expression "slow down and enjoy the journey," and it has eased a daily frustration of mine. We live in a remote area and take a one-lane highway every time we leave or return home. For some reason, most residents in my county seem to drive ten to twenty miles per hour (literally!) under the speed limit on this particular road, which is in extreme contrast to my driving style. I like to think I am a decent driver - I pay attention and focus on the road - but I will admit to having a lead foot every now and then. Suffice to say, my daily drives along this road caused me a great deal of angst.

During the first eighteen months, we lived in our home; I absolutely hated driving along that road. I was on edge every time I turned onto it and would constantly look for opportunities to pass the slower drivers. I wasn't reckless exactly, but there may have been a couple of close calls when I overestimated the distance of an oncoming car. And there were definitely many times when I drove dangerously close to the cars in front of me as if to communicate to the slowpokes in my path that they should put their pedal to the metal.

One day, while driving home behind a particularly slow work van, it struck me that I should take my own advice and look for the positive in the situation. I usually have the kind of optimism that drives others crazy – I quickly find the "silver lining," and my "glass" is always half full. But, for some reason, my positivity failed to kick in during my commutes until it hit me that I was missing an opportunity to slow down and enjoy the journey. As I realized this, I lifted my foot from the gas pedal and backed away from the van ahead of me. I took a deep breath and calmed down, then laughed at myself for allowing something so silly to upset me. After all – what difference would it really make if I arrived home two minutes later? None. But what difference would it make if I hit the van in front of me because I was driving too close? Potentially a great deal – there could be injuries, vehicle damage, insurance claims, and more than two minutes' worth of aggravation at the very least.

The other thing that occurred to me about my frustrating drives along this road is that we should all run our own race and that I should extend more grace to others who are driving their own drive along this particular road and along the road of life. Although I would dearly love people to at least drive the speed limit, I cannot expect everyone to want to. It is not my place to dictate to others the speed they should drive or the speed at which they do anything, but it is my place to be patient and accepting of others and the race they are running.

I should also assume good intent. Since these revelations, I found myself behind a student driver on my way home one day. It was remarkable to me that I was immediately more patient with this particular slow driver than I usually am and that I didn't have to intentionally calm myself and back off the bumper – I did it automatically because I understood that the driver ahead was learning and maybe anxious. So perhaps I should assume that every other driver that irritates me has a valid reason for driving slower than I would like them to. Perhaps I should assume that the driver ahead is elderly and less comfortable with driving than they used to be, or that the driver is simply driving as fast as they feel necessary.

Since that day, I have enjoyed my commutes, and I have learned a few things. I have found that, more often than not, when I relax and accept the situation I find myself in, the slowpokes either magically speed up or turn onto another road, clearing my path. Other times I spot beautiful flowers I have never seen before or a cute bunny in a field, or a spectacular landscape that takes my breath away. I would have missed these sights if my focus was solely fixed on the bumper of the vehicle ahead or the next opportunity to pass. This is a prime example of the wonders of positivity and the fact that happiness begets happiness. The more we smile, the more we have to smile about.

I have also applied this newly acquired realization to other areas in my life where I was slower than usual to find the positive points of a situation. I have found more that more patience has led to more discoveries about the wonders of everyday life that are missed when I am focused on the wrong things – like traffic jams – which are never fun, but which can allow us time to plan; make mental lists; develop goals, or just pump up the jam and have a feel-good singalong. Or long lines in the post office, which may allow us an opportunity to smile at a stranger, wave at a child or have a brief conversation with someone who needed a friendly interaction that day.

Life truly is short, and time truly is precious. By deciding to enjoy the journey, regardless of the circumstances, I find myself in. I can spend more of the priceless moments I have been given in good spirits rather than bad.

Chapter 7 – Snooze you can use

I love taking small steps each day that consistently move me towards my goals and finding ways to incorporate them painlessly into my daily routine. One example of this is doing 20 pushups while waiting for my shower water to warm up, and another is doing squats while swishing my mouthwash in the morning. Both of these are simple and achievable healthy habits that can quickly become second nature when repeated daily.

One of my favorite healthy habits involves the snooze button. No – I don't hit the snooze button over and over again, falling back to sleep each time, avoiding the day ahead until the last possible minute (or second). Each night I set my alarm for a **realistic** (this is key) wake up time the next morning, allowing for one – and only one – snooze period. Each morning I use the one snooze period to do a few things that set me up for a positive day ahead while still in the comfort of my warm cozy bed. When used correctly, this time puts me in a fantastic mood and makes it easy to get up and face anything that life has in store for me in the coming hours.

Here is what I do during the snooze period:

- List three things I am thankful for – I am specific with these thoughts and take the time to visualize them rather than just rush through a list. This lightens my mood and starts my day positively.
- List three things I want to accomplish in the day ahead – again, I am specific with these items to allow my brain to prepare for what is coming. This gives me a head start on being productive because I have already set the wheels in motion for achieving my goals.
- Visualize a great day stretching out before me. I think about my upcoming day, and I imagine it going well. I think about how contented I will feel at the end of the day as I climb back into bed after a day full of positivity and reflect on my successes.

Here is what I don't do during the snooze period:

- Go back to sleep – although I dearly want to some mornings, I have trained myself to use this time to start my day on a positive note with the added bonus of achieving a goal before I even leave my bed.
- Look at my cell phone – I resist this temptation because it can suck me into an hour's worth of scrolling through junk emails and social media posts (neither of which are a good use of the first precious minutes of my day).
- Allow any negative thoughts to creep in – I refuse to focus on anything negative during this time to allow myself the best chance of remaining positive throughout the rest of the day. If I anticipate any challenges ahead, I resolve then and there that I will handle them well.

I find that my mood is brighter, and my days are more productive when I use the snooze time to focus on the positivity in my life and the wonder that lays before me in the day ahead. It is a great investment of a few minutes in the morning with a payoff of happiness that lasts for hours. It may be helpful to use a notebook to write down your thoughts each day. Many experts believe that things stick with us longer when we take the extra step to document them.

One other note to make on this subject is that it is counter-active to set an alarm time for much earlier than you actually need it. When we set a realistic morning alarm, we have more quality sleep than if we hit the snooze button five times, dozing off in between, and we accomplish a goal before even getting out of bed - which is a fantastic start to a positive day.

Chapter 8 – If you're happy and you know it…

We all want to be happy. When I surveyed my Facebook friends, 93% of the responders said they would rather be happy than rich. We certainly want our loved ones to be happy, and most of us even want complete strangers to be happy.

But we're not happy.

As a society, we are increasingly angry, depressed, negative, and critical. There are some among us who are truly happy, but they seem to be few and far between. We spend huge amounts of money on self-help books and therapy and "stuff" to make us happy, but it doesn't seem to be working. So, are we predisposed to being more or less happy, or is it something we can cultivate within ourselves? I believe we can learn to be happy and that our happiness can inspire others to seek it too. In fact, I have a plan to help us find the happiness that seems so difficult to capture, along with an acronym to help make it easy to remember.

> H – Help
> A – Appreciate
> P – Positivity
> P – Power
> Y – Yippee

The H stands for help and reminds us to help others. Research has shown over and over again that helping others makes us feel good about ourselves, which in turn makes us happy. According to Psychology Today, "the positive energy that you feel from doing a good deed can act on your body in much the same way that exercise does, releasing endorphins that make you feel good naturally." This doesn't mean you should stop exercising, but it does explain the "helpers high" that we feel when we help others and why we should do it more often. Buddha said this: "if you light a lamp for somebody, it will also brighten your path." I offer a word of caution here: don't forget to help yourself too – you can't pour from an empty cup and will be unable to help anyone if you become run down and overwhelmed.

The A stands for appreciate and reminds us that gratitude is the best attitude. It is impossible to feel any negative emotion when we are completely focused on our blessings. Try it for just a minute – think of something you are truly grateful for and pay attention to the warm fuzzy feeling that envelopes you. In this state, all other emotions slip away and leave us. You can't possibly be angry when you focus on the simple fact that you are able to read this when millions of people across the world have impaired vision. One of my favorite quotes is: "there is always, always something to be thankful for," and, even on a bad day, I know you can find something – no matter how small – to appreciate. On the day my stepfather passed away, we were grateful that he had been given the time to marry my mum in his final days, which is something she will always cherish.

The first P stands for positivity and reminds us to focus on what is going well rather than what is not. When we search for it, we can find positivity everywhere. Have you noticed that when you buy a new car, you suddenly see that make and model everywhere? It's because it has now become important to you and your brain looks for it. Positivity can work the same way – if you make it important, then your brain will look for it. Do you know a particularly positive person? If so, make efforts to spend more time with them, and their upbeat characteristics will rub off on you. Observe them as they talk and consciously make efforts to mirror their reactions and their traits – they will become natural to you over time if you repeat them often enough.

The second P stands for power and reminds us that we can choose to be happy, no matter what is going on around us. We have the power to determine how we will react to rude people or disappointments, or negativity. I, for one, refuse to give anyone else that kind of power over my life. We can truly decide – even in the midst of dark days – to focus on the brightness in life and to remain happy in spite of the circumstances. Abraham Lincoln said this: "most folks are about as happy as they make up their minds to be." Happy people simply want to be happy and generally don't allow the bad stuff the power to affect them as much as unhappy people do. This is another habit that can be adopted with intention by intentionally focusing on our thoughts and becoming aware when the negativity or anger creeps into our minds. As soon as we recognize these occurring, we can remind ourselves that we have the power over our thoughts and actions and that we can choose to be happy every minute of every day.

The Y is my favorite. It stands for "YIPPEE" and reminds us to celebrate. Oprah said this: "the more you celebrate your life, the more there is to celebrate." I believe it is important to celebrate our victories – both big and small – and those of the people around us. When we acknowledge the good in life, the bad bits don't seem quite so bad, so find something to celebrate every single day. When you find a good parking spot at the mall, allow yourself a quick "YIPPEE." When you are given a compliment, have a "YIPPEE" (you might want to keep this one quiet). When you scratch something off your to-do list, say "YIPPEE." There are so many small victories we can celebrate, and it is fun to acknowledge them. Don't forget to spread happiness by celebrating the victories of others – and watch their surprise when you yell "YIPPEE" unexpectedly. One more thing – kids LOVE to celebrate, so make sure you get them involved wherever possible. You could implement a daily celebration conversation at the dinner table where each family member shares something to celebrate about their day (bonus points if you can get teenagers involved, and double bonus if you can get everyone to yell "YIPPEE). If that doesn't make you happy, I don't know what will.

Chapter 9 – Rewrite the script

No pain, no gain.

Bad things happen to good people.

The best is yet to come.

Another day another dollar.

Each of these expressions, and many more, rattle around our head and are spoken aloud countless times each day. We have become so familiar with numerous expressions such as these that they are repeated without a second thought. But if we do stop and give them a second thought, we may realize they could potentially send negative messages to others and, more importantly, to ourselves.

Let's take a look at the first expression above: "no pain, no gain." In theory, these words are meant to convey that – although the present is painful – the future will be brighter. But there is a strong possibility that they have become so ingrained in our culture and in our own minds that we are convinced that we can't possibly have that bright future unless we first endure pain. Taken a step further, if we find ourselves in a good place without previous suffering, can we allow ourselves to enjoy happiness? Is it real if we didn't sacrifice to obtain it? Do we deserve it without first paying the price?

"Bad things happen to good people" implies that only the best of us is meant to suffer. Again, at first glance, these words are not harmful – they have been used to comfort others when life becomes difficult. But are we allowing this expression to lead us to expect the bad times? By repeating these words, are we inviting the bad events into our lives? Are we setting ourselves up for the bad things because our subconscious mind is already looking for them if we believe that good people are supposed to suffer them?

"The best is yet to come" is used to encourage us during both good and bad times. When the going gets tough, this expression reassures us that the good stuff is right around the corner, but we may need to suffer a little first before we reach it. When we are on top of the world, these words inspire us to reach even higher for even bigger and better results and outcomes and to want more and more. However, my fear is that these words may teach us that we cannot find happiness during the dark days and that we should not be satisfied with happiness during the bright days.

The term "another day, another dollar" is often used at work or to refer to our work. It conveys a "here we go again" sort of attitude, as though we are resigned to the daily grind without much enthusiasm. Work can be challenging – in fact; it can be downright soul-destroying (I should know – I left my job of 22 years because my values were compromised). However, once again, we have a choice each and every day to smile and make the best of the hours we have been given, rather than resign ourselves to drudgery. If we need to work to pay the bills (let's face it – most of us do), then why not enjoy it? If we don't like the job/boss/company/career we find ourselves in, then why not change it?

I think it is time to create new and positive versions of many of the scripts that circle through our brains.

The first step is to recognize the words we tell ourselves. Pay attention to the words that pop into your mind as you go about your life. Take note of the expressions that occur to you to use in the act of comforting and encouraging others, as well as those you use to reassure yourself. The second step is to analyze the words and make sure they don't contain a negative message, no matter how well-intended they are. The third step is to rewrite the script. Change the expressions to ensure they are positive and pure and that the meaning truly matches the message.

Here are some rewritten expressions to try out:

The ~~best~~ REST is yet to come – the rest of your story will play out, there will be highs and lows along the way, but now is the time to be happy – regardless of where you find yourself.

No ~~pain~~ GRIT, no gain – grit is strength and determination in difficult times. Grit is making a choice to keep moving forward. Grit is within our control, whereas pain may not be.

~~Bad~~ ALL things happen to ~~good~~ ALL people – each of us will endure the good, the bad, and the ugly along the journey of life, and we should embrace each season and the lessons within them.

Another day, another ~~dollar~~ DELIGHT – each new day brings a new chance to be happy and to make others happy, and a new opportunity to live a life of joy.

Chapter 10 – Be happy, healthy, and kind one day at a time

Set-up Sunday

The dreaded Monday morning alarm clock is less of a shock to the system when we dedicate some time on Sunday to prepare for the chaos of the coming week. One of my favorite proverbs demonstrates the importance of this action: "A Sunday well spent brings a week of content." The success of your week depends on how well you prepare for it, and I find that my week goes much smoother when I have set aside time on Sunday to get organized. Here are some ideas to get you started:

- It is all too easy to order take-out or resort to fast food when faced with the "what's for dinner" dilemma after a long day. Grocery shopping and meal prepping on Sundays allow for cheaper and healthier meal options.
- A good night's sleep on Sunday helps me hit the ground running on Monday, so I try to resist the temptation of staying up late and squeezing the last few drops out of the weekend.
- Coordinate the upcoming week's family activity schedules. Discuss the appointments, "drop offs" and "pickups" ahead of time to avoid a last-minute scramble.
- Make a weekly to-do list on a Sunday for random tasks such as scheduling doctor appointments, oil changes, or buying a birthday present for a party the following weekend.
- Non-perishable items can be organized for the Monday through Friday lunch boxes to lessen daily work.
- Catch up on the laundry, so there is no need for a midnight load when something is needed urgently.

Money Monday

In order to be truly healthy, we must monitor our physical, emotional, spiritual, mental, and financial health, and we will focus on financial health on Mondays as an important aspect of our overall health. There are several small but impactful tasks we can complete in a short time to improve our financial health.

- Consider balancing your checkbook or checking your credit card statement to make sure there aren't any lingering automatic drafts for subscriptions or memberships you no longer use.
- Review your beneficiaries to ensure they are still appropriate as relationships change over time, or even take steps to make a will.
- Call the cable company and lower your monthly bill - maybe you really don't need that premium package with the extra 200 channels and six receivers.
- I pack my lunch most workdays because I am a self-proclaimed cheapskate, but doing so just one day a week can lead to a huge amount of savings over the course of a year when you consider the average price of a fast-food meal is now around $7.00 ($7.00 x 52 = $364).
- Take this a step further and have a total "no spend" day: make coffee at home instead of driving through Starbucks; pack your lunch; skip the store on the way home and shop for dinner in your freezer or pantry; and avoid amazon when you get home in the evening.
- Contact a financial advisor to review your long-term goals (I can help you find one in your area).

Trash Tuesday

Tuesday is the day to simplify and de-clutter an area of your life. From the obvious to the obscure, we can spend a few minutes improving our mental health today by eliminating the waste that bogs us down.

- Pick one room and remove one bag of trash – unworn clothes in the dresser and closet, out-of-date food in the kitchen pantry, and freezer expired medicines, and unused make-up in the bathroom (don't forget to donate all appropriate items).
- Tackle the dreaded junk drawer or Tupperware cupboard – there is bound to be enough in these areas to fill a trash bag.

- If you're like me, your car is a dumping ground for empty soda cans, snack wrappers, and other trash. There may or may not have been a donation bag in my trunk for the last three months.
- Make an effort on Tuesdays to clean out your inbox. I receive countless junk emails each day that I need to unsubscribe to but never seem to make the time.
- Purge your social media accounts – do you really need to know what your best friend's cousin's mother-in-law is having for dinner tonight, or what grades your ex-neighbor's brother's bratty kid scored on his 3rd-grade report card?
- I spend way more time than I care to admit watching trash TV. Although it's a pleasant way to unwind after a harrowing day, I dare say I could achieve the same results by reading a book and gain the added benefits of broadening my mind rather than numbing it.
- Focus on your thoughts and trash the negative ones. Begin the habit of allowing positive affirmations to replace any negativity that crosses our minds.

Workout Wednesday

Ideally, we should engage in physical activity multiple times per week, but many people insist they don't have time to exercise. I get it – life is busy. What if we chose just one day each week to find the time to be active – is it possible we might actually enjoy it enough to commit to doing more?

- In just five minutes, you can complete 50-second rounds of five different exercises with 10 seconds of rest in between (consider push-ups, squats, sit-ups, burpees, and a plank to really get the blood pumping).
- Spend ten minutes stretching out your muscle groups.
- My company encourages staff to get up and walk around the office at 3 pm every Wednesday – this is more effective than caffeine at beating the hump day slump.
- Choose the stairs rather than the elevator on Wednesdays.

- I love to walk but rarely take the time these days. Did you know that just 30 minutes of walking on a regular basis can alleviate depression, limit chronic disease, improve blood pressure, lower the risk of heart disease, and keep weight in check? There are so many options for this FREE exercise: you can walk in place; on a treadmill; outside; and even in a mall on rainy days (don't laugh – I've done it – just don't take your wallet with you, or you may be tempted to shop).

Thankful Thursday

"There is always, always something to be thankful for," author unknown. This is so very true. Even on our darkest days, we can find something we appreciate. When my stepfather lost his battle with cancer, we were grateful that he had been able to marry my mum during his last days. During a particularly bleak day of raising a challenging teenage boy, I was reminded by a friend that her son didn't live long enough to drive her crazy during the teenage years. It is also true that when we focus on the things we have; we focus less on the things we don't have.

- Today, let's be thankful for our health. Even those in poor health may have the ability to see and hear.
- We should be thankful for our family, friends, and the people who add meaning to our lives.
- Unlike many, I am blessed to live in a warm (or cool – depending on the season) home with running water, food in the pantry, and clothes in the closet.
- Remind yourself that you "get to" work, when so many are jobless, rather than "have to" work.
- Spend time to appreciate the fact that you were given another chance at life when you woke up this morning. You can make a difference in your own life and in the lives of others today. You can love and be loved today. You can create more memories today.

Feel-good Friday

Today's world can be a dark place for many people who are struggling to put one foot in front of the other and keep going. We don't always know which of the people surrounding us are having a bad day, week, or month. This is just one of the countless reasons to be kind every single day to every single person in every single circumstance. I propose making a special effort on Friday's to perform a random act of kindness to make someone else feel good. Complete strangers or dear friends alike can benefit from your kindness, and the best news is that you will also feel good. The term "helpers high" refers to the warm fuzzy feelings you get after helping someone, and these feelings can actually improve the state of our physical, mental, and emotional health.

- Pay a compliment, hold a door, smile, or greet a stranger warmly. You can allow someone to go ahead of you in a grocery store line or a line of traffic. Kindness does not have to be costly.
- I love the feel-good stories about people "paying it forward" in fast food lines. I recently heard about a lady whose order was prepaid by the person in front of her and, when she offered to pay for the order behind her, she was surprised to learn this had been happening for two hours. Kindness is contagious!
- Donate your time, money, or skills to any number of good causes – from your local animal or homeless shelters to nursing homes and fire stations.
- Send a note to thank someone you appreciate.
- Take snacks to work and watch your colleagues smile – I have found that nothing spreads faster in an office than news of free food.

Spoil yourself Saturday

We sometimes forget to be kind to ourselves, and we often don't take the time to take care of ourselves. Just as airplane oxygen masks should be applied to ourselves first in order to help others, we are able to spread more kindness when we are happy. It is so important that we slow down and recharge our batteries on a regular basis, but this simple act is easy to forget as we rush through life. Taking even a small amount of time for self-care can produce huge impacts on our health and happiness.

- Spend some time today doing exactly what YOU want, rather than doing what everyone else wants.
- Read a book and lose yourself in a fantasy world where your worries don't exist.
- Take a nap and wake up refreshed, ready to face whatever life has in store for you.
- Go shopping for something you WANT rather than something you NEED (within reason, of course).
- Indulge in a warm bubble bath, a quiet coffee alone, or "that" TV show that you don't readily admit to watching in public.

What will you do to "be happy, healthy and kind" today?

Conclusion

Happiness is contagious. Happiness leads to better health, better relationships, and even better jobs.

We get what we focus on – this has been said many times, in many forms, by many people – and I believe this to be true without a shadow of a doubt. So, focus on becoming a happyist and you will become a happyist. Focus on other happyists, and on happyist habits to help you along the way.

I leave you with this final thought: have you ever noticed that the happiest people are often the ones who carry the biggest burdens? Many of the happiest people I know struggle with disabilities or illness or pain, and yet they sparkle, they enjoy the journey, and they spread joy. This may be the biggest lesson of all.

www.ingramcontent.com/pod-product-compliance
Lightning Source LLC
Chambersburg PA
CBHW051937150726
47999CB00006B/2263